a M. Lee

Let's Explore
UNDERWATER

Written by
Steve Parker

Illustrated by
David Anstey

COLLINS

William Collins Sons & Co Ltd
London • Glasgow • Sydney • Auckland
Toronto • Johannesburg

First published in Great Britain in 1990
by William Collins Sons & Co Ltd
Devised and produced by Templar Publishing Co Ltd
Pippbrook Mill, London Road, Dorking, Surrey RH4 1JE

A CIP Catalogue record for this book is available from the British Library.

Editor Andy Charman
Designer Jane Hunt
Colour separations by Positive Colour Ltd, Maldon, Essex
Printed and bound by MacLehose & Partners, England

ISBN 0 00 185323 6 (hardback)
ISBN 0 00 185324 4 (paperback)

CONTENTS

What is water?

Water is almost everywhere on our planet. It is in the air we breathe – in the form of invisible gas called water vapour. It floats across the sky as clouds and can fall to the earth as rain, hail and snow. It is in the soil, as a film of moisture coating every particle. It collects to form streams, ponds, rivers, lakes and seas.

Land animals like us are familiar with different ***habitats*** *(places to live) on land, such as forests, deserts, moorlands and grasslands. Underwater habitats are also amazingly varied. There are mountains and valleys, cliffs and plains, sunlit 'gardens' of plants and dark, mysterious caves. Although an ocean and a pond are both made of water, they are very different worlds.*

HOW MUCH WATER?

More than seven-tenths of our world is covered by water. Nearly all of this is sea water. Fresh water, such as ponds and lakes, makes up only 0.1 percent or one-thousandth of the water on our planet. Huge amounts of fresh water are solid, frozen into ice, towering high above the sea at the Poles and on many high mountains.

Water is......

Chemist:
'A drop of water is made of billions of identical *molecules*. Each molecule is formed of two hydrogen *atoms* joined to one oxygen atom. So the chemical formula for water is H_2O.'

Biologist:
'Life began in water, in prehistoric seas. In our bodies, the chemicals that keep us alive are dissolved in water. Without it, life would cease.'

Physicist:
'Water is the most common substance on earth. It has no colour, taste, or smell. At ordinary temperatures it is liquid. It turns to ice below 0°C and to water vapour above 100°C.'

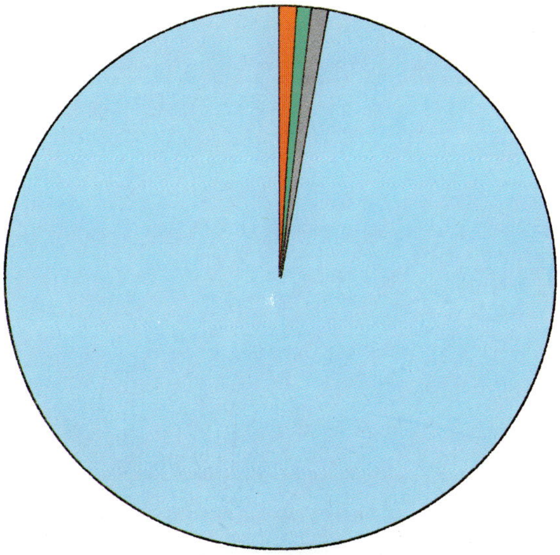

Water in rocks, underground rivers, caves, etc.

Water as streams, rivers, lakes

Salty water in seas and oceans

Frozen glacial ice

The pie chart above shows how the total amount of water on earth, 1,321 million cubic kilometres, is divided up into sea and fresh water.

What would happen?

The great southern continent of Antarctica is covered by an enormous ice cap more than 1500 metres thick. Many scientists predict that the world's temperature will rise because of the 'greenhouse effect'. **If this came to pass, what do you think might happen to Antarctica?**

ANSWERS

WHAT WOULD HAPPEN?
If the world's temperature rises enough, Antarctica's ice cap might start to melt. The water would run into the sea and raise the sea level. If all the ice melted, the sea level would go up by about 60 metres – a terrifying thought!

Water on the move

Water is not easily created or destroyed by physical or chemical processes. The same water has been on our planet for millions of years. But it is always on the move. If water is on a slope, it is pulled down by the force of ***gravity****. This is why water 'flows' or 'runs'. The reason may seem obvious as you watch a stream rushing down a mountainside. But water is still sliding down a slope – although a less steep one – when it flows slowly along a large river.*

THE WATER CYCLE

The same water goes around and around in a process called the *water cycle*. Here are some of the main parts of the cycle. Water falls to the Earth in the form of rain, snow and hail. **How does it get back up again?** Clue: look in the sky to find out!

Fast or slow?

The Earth's surface is gradually changing. Old mountains are worn away and huge rock movements buckle the Earth's surface. As the Earth changes, the pattern of water flow alters. New areas of land come under water and others dry out. Animals and plants living in the running water of a river may eventually find themselves in the still water of an ox-bow lake or a backwater, or stagnant pool.

The ox-bow lake

1. As a river flows in a wide loop, the fast currents on the outside of the curve wear away parts of its banks.

2. Over many years the loop in the river becomes more and more pronounced.

3. Eventually, the river takes a new course and part is cut off to become an ox-bow lake.

The billabong

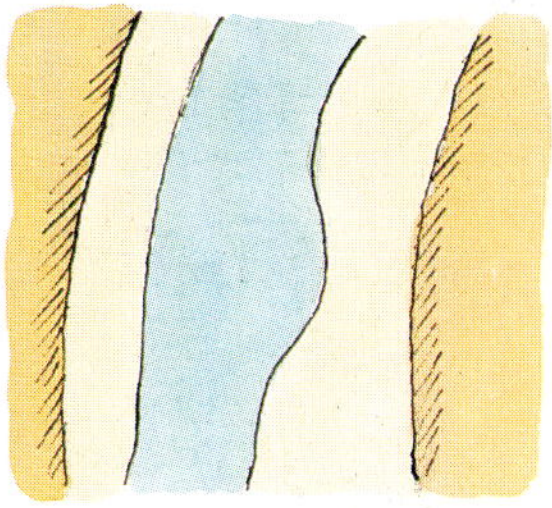

1. In the dry season, a river slowly shrinks.

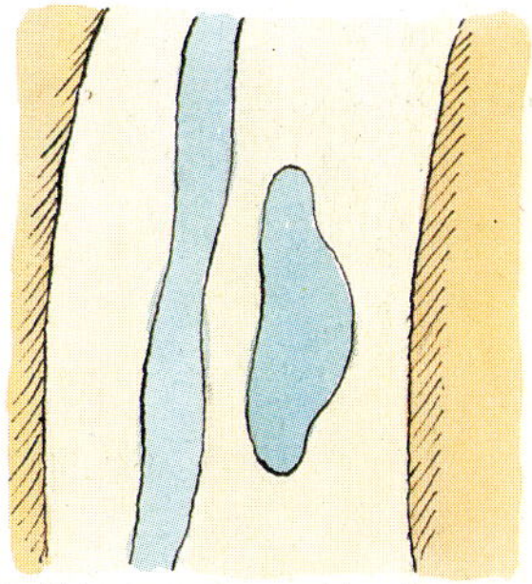

2. Water trapped in deep holes in its bed becomes isolated from the main flow. These separated pools are called billabongs or backwaters.

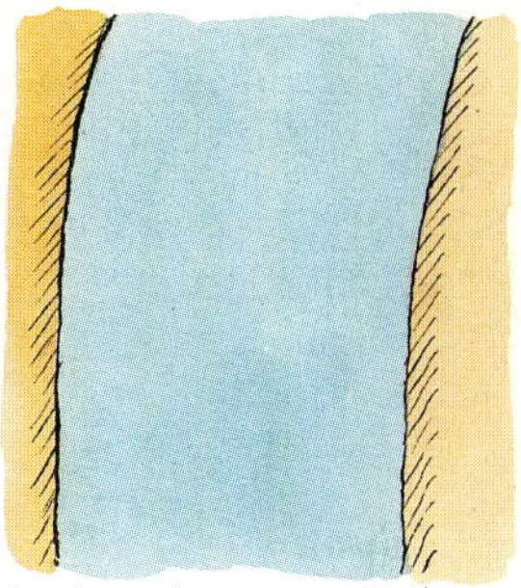

3. In the rainy season, the river level rises and covers them again.

ANSWERS

THE WATER CYCLE

The driving force behind the water cycle is the Sun! The Sun's heat rays warm the water and some of it evaporates, that is, turns from liquid to gas. This gaseous water is warmer than the surrounding air and so it floats up into the sky. You can see this every day, as a puddle of rain water dries out. It is also happening all day, every day, on rivers, lakes and oceans across the world.

Moving under water

*Moving through air is usually easy, although it is hard to move against a strong wind. Moving through water is much more difficult because it is 'thicker' or denser than air. We say that it offers more **resistance** to the moving object.*

*Water offers less resistance to bodies that are long and thin. This is called **streamlining**, and it enables a fish to swim faster. We can guess whether an underwater creature is a fast or slow mover from the shape of its body.*

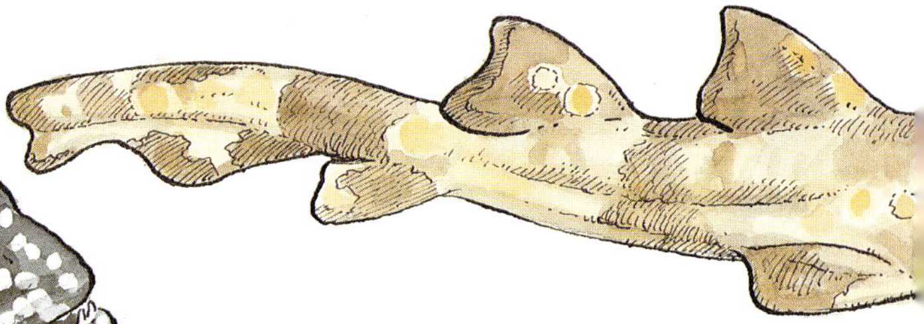

QUEENSLAND GROUPER

This deep-bodied, heavily-built fish grows to 3 metres long and weighs more than three people. It lurks around the reefs and jetties of Australia's east coast. Built not for speed but for strength, the **grouper** (or **groper**) tends to ambush its prey. It creeps around a rock and then snaps up the victim in its vast mouth.

GREAT BARRACUDA

This super-streamlined sea fish cruises the warm waters of the Caribbean, on the lookout for smaller fish. When it spots a likely prey, the **barracuda** flicks its mighty 3-metre-long body and darts through the water to catch the victim in its sharp teeth.

Fast or slow?

The big fish above are all sea-dwellers. However, freshwater fish also have body shapes that give clues to their lifestyle. **Can you pair each of these freshwater fish with a sea-dwelling fish of a similar kind?**

Zander This is a long, slim fish from Europe that grows up to just over a metre in length.

Wels This flat-bodied creature, also called the **European catfish**, grows up to 3 metres long.

Carp The **European common carp** has a strong, thick-set body and a wide mouth. The biggest carp are about 1 metre long.

WOBBEGONG SHARK

This shark from the Australasia region has a flattened body. It lies on the sea bed. To the animals it hunts, it probably resembles a seaweed-encrusted rock. As a careless creature swims past, the 2.5-metre-long **wobbegong** rises, snatches it and gulps it down.

Record-breakers!

Stories differ on which animal is the fastest underwater swimmer, because it is not easy to measure the speed of a wild creature. Here are some underwater record-breakers and the speeds they can reach. Note how sleek and highly streamlined they are.

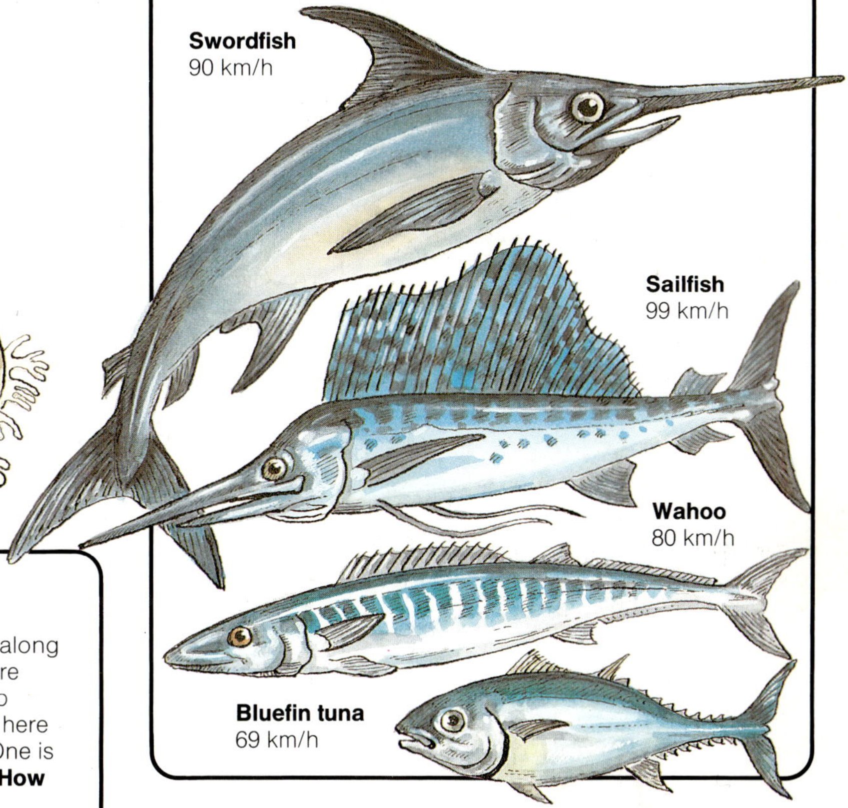

What pushes the water?

On land, animals use their legs to push themselves along the ground. Underwater, broad, flat-shaped limbs are more effective in pushing water backwards – and so propelling the body forwards. The creatures shown here belong to different groups in the animal kingdom. One is an *amphibian*, one is a bird and one is a mammal. **How do they move along?**

ANSWERS

FAST OR SLOW?

The **wels** is a mostly bottom-dwelling fish, like the **wobbegong**. It scavenges along lake and river beds for dead and dying creatures, and it also eats shellfish and small fish.

The **zander** is a streamlined predator, like the **barracuda**. It hunts smaller fish of all kinds.

The **carp** has a similar lifestyle to the **grouper**. It lives in weedy lakes and grubs in the mud for freshwater insects, shellfish and water plants.

WHAT PUSHES THE WATER?

The **frog** kicks its long, powerful back legs and its webbed feet propel it forwards.

The **penguin** has evolved oar-shaped wings and 'rows' along under the water.

The **seal** also rows itself, using its front limbs or 'arms'.

Almost swept away

The stream is the 'windiest' place in the underwater world. On land, very strong winds can uproot trees and blow away any animal caught out in the open. Underwater, the stream's current acts in the same way. Sometimes it is not so powerful. In dry weather the stream shrinks to a gentle brook, and parts of the bed dry out. But after rain, or as winter snows melt, it becomes a rushing torrent that tumbles pebbles, and boulders along its bed, carrying away anything that is not firmly attached. For stream animals, life is a continual battle against the speed and power of moving water, and the dangers of the current.

Who's who in the stream?

Animals cope with the current in different ways. Some are clingers, hanging on to pebbles with strong claws. Some are suckers, with fleshy lobes that suck down onto the rock. Some are hiders, waiting in cracks and holes for the current to carry food along to them. Others are swimmers, with powerful paddling limbs or sinuous wriggling bodies that can propel them against all but the fastest-flowing water. Look at the stream scene shown here. **How do the eight animals from various parts of the world cope with the current?**

1. The **desman** has large back legs with webbed toes. It hunts at night for insects and other small water animals.
2. The **olive mayfly** *larva* (grub or nymph) has a broad, flat head and body, and its legs end in sharp hooked claws.
3. The **stonefly** larva has a flattened body and broad claws Later, it will leave the water and turn into an adult fly.
4. The **caddis fly** larva spins a fine silky net strung between small stones.
5. The **water snake** can move its body vigorously from side to side. It hunts frogs, fish and small mammals.
6. The **horse leech** has a worm-like body with a soft pad under each end. It swallows tiny creatures whole.
7. The **freshwater shrimp** is flattened from side to side. If caught out in the open water it may be swept away.
8. The **flatworm** glides along slowly leaving a sticky trail of slime behind it.

GOING FOR A DIP?

Dippers are small birds that live by fast-flowing streams. They not only fly well, they can also dive and swim, and they can walk underwater! The dipper makes its way along the stream bed, pecking among stones for water insects and other food. Often it walks upstream, head down against the current. Dippers can often be seen standing on streamside boulders, bobbing up and down with 'dipping' movements. In fact, this is how they got their name.

GIANT OF THE EASTERN STREAMS

Salamanders are amphibians, related to **newts** and **frogs**. Some kinds of salamanders live in streams, preying on small *aquatic* animals ('aquatic' means 'living in water'). In Europe they are mostly small, about 10–20 cm long. The biggest is the **Chinese giant salamander**, which grows up to 2 metres long! It hunts at night in cold hill streams and marshes, hiding behind a rock or root and seizing food with a sideways swipe of the head.

ANSWERS

WHO'S WHO IN THE STREAM

Net-spinning caddis This caddis larva is a hider, staying in the shelter of stones or weed. The net that it spins traps food brought by the current.

Stonefly larva One of the best clingers, with sprawling limbs that keep its body down on the stones and give it a good grip.

Desman The desman is a powerful swimmer and chases after prey by kicking its back feet.

Horse leech A good sucker that can 'loop' along like a caterpillar, using first its front sucker and then its rear one.

Water snake Although it has no limbs, the water snake is an excellent swimmer. It throws its body into S-shaped curves and slides smoothly through the water.

Olive mayfly larva An accomplished clinger, with six wide-set legs that provide a broad base for hanging on.

Flatworm The flatworm is a clinger. The whole of its body acts as a sucker and slug-like slime gives it an even better grip.

Freshwater shrimp This hider's narrow body enables it to squeeze into cracks and crevices. It feeds on decaying debris among the stones.

Life under the surface

*The pond is an underwater world in miniature. Under its calm surface the struggles of life and death, which take place in any other natural habitat, are occurring. Plants are busy growing, **herbivores** (plant-eaters) are consuming the plants, **omnivores** are eating plants and animals, and **carnivores** (meat-eaters) are hunting other animals and even each other.*

Where do they feed?

The pond is organized in 'layers', each type of animal or plant living in the place that suits it best. **Can you figure out where these creatures usually live based on what they eat?**

Backswimmer Detects vibrations passing through the surface film of the water. Its prey may be a drowning fly, a tadpole, or a small fish.

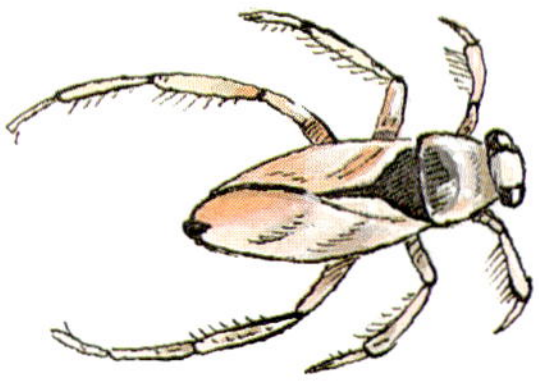

Dragonfly larva Hides in the mud or under leaves. The larva feeds using a hinged and hooked lower jaw, which it 'shoots' at its victim.

PROBLEMS FOR POND PLANTS

The first flowering plants evolved on land. Egg cells are *fertilized* by *pollen* carried from other plants by animals or the wind. Later, the seeds are dispersed in the same way. In the stillness of a pond, flowering plants have to find other ways of doing this. Here are some of the ways in which aquatic plants have tackled such difficulties.

TINY BUDDERS

Duckweed plants are very small. The 'leaf' is not a true leaf but a plant part called a *thallus*. This can send out buds which quickly grow into new thalli. In this way duckweed quickly carpets a pond's surface, without the need for pollen or seeds.

SPRAWLING STEMS

The **lesser water parsnip** has side stems called *stolons*. These bend down under their own weight as they grow longer. Where they touch the pond bottom, they give out roots and grow into new plants.

Great diving beetle Clasps plant stems with its middle pair of legs. It uses its front legs and fearsome jaws to catch tadpoles, small fish and other prey as they swim past.

Frog Lies in wait for small creatures such as flies, worms and slugs, which it catches by flicking out its long, sticky tongue.

ANSWERS

WHERE DO THEY FEED?

Backswimmer This water bug hangs just under the surface of the water. It may attack a moth or fly that has fallen into the water.

Great diving beetle This terror of the small pond either clings to plant stems or roams about looking for its victims. It usually hunts in the midwater to bottom region.

Dragonfly larva This hungry hunter lives in the mud and therefore favours the bottom of the pond. Sometimes it may climb a plant stem to lurk in the leaves and ambush swimmers-by.

Frog That was a trick question! Frogs do not usually live under the water in ponds. They tend to hang around the pond's edge or in damp grass and vegetation nearby. They generally go under the water only during early spring, when they breed.

FLOWERS IN AIR

The **water lily** has a long stem anchored in the mud at the bottom of the pond, but its flowers float above the water's surface. This means that insects can transfer pollen from flower to flower.

TRUE WATER PLANTS

Hornwort grows completely underwater. Male flowers produce small 'floats' containing pollen. These come loose and rise to the surface, where they break open. The pollen floats down through the water, to land on the female flowers.

An underwater home

*As streams join together to become a river, the underwater world changes. The river is a rich natural habitat. Many animals, from fish to **crayfish** to water birds and **otters**, make their home there. The current is not so fierce. Plants can take root along the banks without being washed away, and they provide shelter and food. Out in the wide water there is more room to swim around. One animal goes so far as to change part of the river into a home that's even more to its liking. This is the **beaver**, which builds a dam and creates its own lake.*

WHY MAKE A LAKE?

Beavers live in family groups of a male, female and their young. Here is the family at work on its dams, its *lodge* (home) and its system of pools and canals. The lake created by the beavers' efforts keeps the surrounding area moist, encouraging the growth of water plants and trees. It also keeps the entrance to their house underwater. **How do these two things help the beavers?** (Look in the background for a clue!)

The lodge is safe in the middle of the lake. It is strongly constructed and very difficult to dig through.

The lodge entrance is under the water, which allows the beavers to leave the lodge in winter by swimming under the surface ice.

ANSWERS

WHY MAKE A LAKE?

A lake provides food and a safe place to live. It encourages the growth of water-plants, damp-loving ferns and waterside trees like **willow** and **aspen** – all favourite foods of the beaver. The strongly-built lodge with its underwater entrance is a good defence against the predators that live in beaver country – such as that **wolf** hiding in the bushes!

WHOSE HOME?

The **stickleback's** home is the nest of twigs and leaves. Here his partner lays her eggs, and here he guards them as they hatch and grow into tiny fish that can dart back into the nest for safety.

The **caddis fly** larva makes a home by gluing together particles of sand and shell. This protects its soft body.

The **water spider's** home is the bubble. It spins a web in the water-weeds and fills it with air, collected from the surface of the water as tiny bubbles of air.

The beaver gnaws through the trunks of small trees using its sharp front teeth. These are used as food and for dam-building.

Beavers eat water plants, ferns, bark and twigs from riverside trees. Twigs are stored in underwater 'larders' for the winter.

Stones, mud and sticks are wedged and woven into a waterproof wall – the dam.

Whose home?

Here are three more animals and three more underwater 'homes', made for various purposes. **Can you match each home to its builder?**

Stickleback male guards his baby fish as they hatch

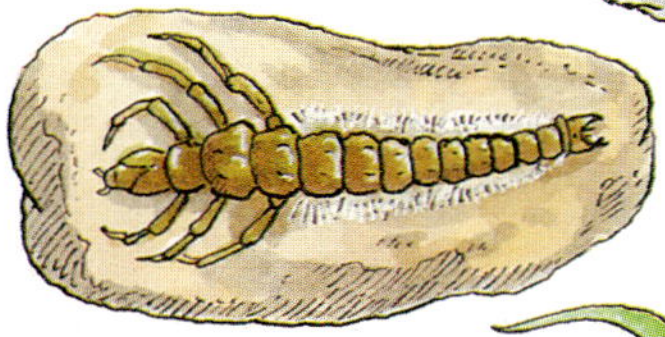

Caddis fly larva's body is long, soft and vulnerable

Water spider has no gills and breathes air

1. Home of tiny bits of sand and shells glued into a tube

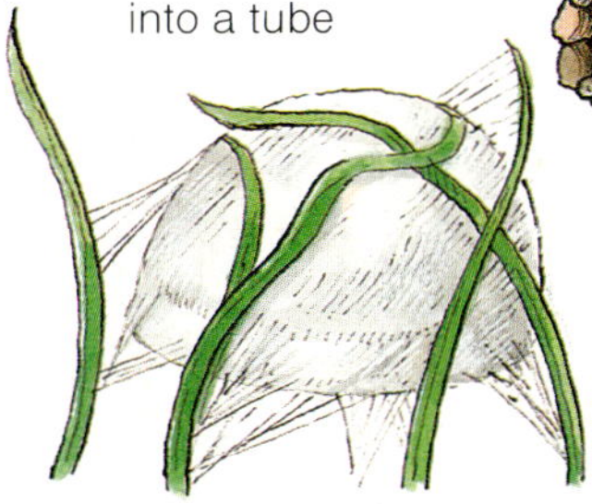

2. Home of a large air bubble trapped under a silken net

3. Home of small twigs, leaves and other vegetation

Water-what?

When is a rat a **water rat**? When it's in the water! The name 'water rat' is often given to any rat-like animal swimming in a pond or river. This could be one of three different animals.

It might be a **brown rat**. This adaptable animal swims well and eats mainly plants.

It could be a **water vole**, which has a blunt head, a thick glossy coat and a body about 20 cm long.

It may be a **water shrew**. This tiny hunter feeds mainly on insect larvae and worms, and its body is 7.5 cm long

'Islands' of water

*A small island in the middle of the ocean may seem like an isolated place to us. But for animals that live underwater, a lake is like an isolated 'island' in a 'sea' of land. Unless there are rivers along which they can swim, lake animals are trapped. Because of this, fish such as the **cichlids** from African lakes can show us how **evolution** works. In true detective style, scientists have pieced together clues given by the fish themselves, and from the **geology**, or structure, of the rocks in the region, to show how new species evolve.*

Monsters in the lakes!

Large lakes, deep and dark and silent, have long excited people's imagination. All over the world there are legends about lake monsters. One of the most famous of these is about the Loch Ness monster from Scotland. This creature is said to resemble a **plesiosaur**, a type of prehistoric reptile.

Haplochromis euchilus is an insect-eating cichlid from Lake Malawi. Its mouthparts are small and tube-like for sucking up small creatures.

EVOLUTION IN ACTION

Lakes such as Victoria, Malawi and Tanganyika, in East Africa, were not always large individual lakes. Over one million years ago they probably consisted of a few small lakes and rivers. Only a few species of cichlids lived there.

Over thousands of years, earth movements and changes in the climate caused new lakes to form. In

This vicious predator, **Haplochromis compressiceps**, has a large mouth with rows of sharp teeth for catching and eating its prey.

Pseudotropheus zebra comes from Lake Malawi. It has a hard, horny mouth for rasping small water plants from rocks.

Perissodus microlepis has tiny blade-like teeth, for nipping scales off other fish. It comes from Lake Tanganyika.

each new lake, the fish evolved to suit their surroundings and became different from the fish in other lakes. Today, these lakes are homes to hundreds of different species of cichlids. Each species is unique in the way that it lives. This means that the different types of fish do not compete for the same food or space in the lake.

Fish meals

Compare the fish shown here to the cichlids in the main picture. Although they come from different parts of the world, they are similar in certain ways, because of the food they eat. **Can you match each fish with its meal?**

ANSWERS

FISH MEALS

Food 1 is eaten by the **bream**. It uses its tube-like mouth to suck up the mud and swallow the creatures in it.

Food 2 is eaten by the **pike**. This fierce hunter snaps up its unwary prey with its very sharp teeth.

Food 3 is eaten by the **parrotfish**. This fish's beak is ideal for scraping weeds from underwater rocks.

Fresh and salty

Fresh water and sea water look much the same, but for underwater animals and plants, the difference is enormous. Sea water contains a substance called sodium chloride, better known as salt. This greatly affects the body chemistry, so sea creatures have evolved bodies that can cope with this saltiness or ***salinity****. This is why sea animals cannot live in lakes, and vice versa. Where fresh water and salt water meet, you will find the ever-changing world of the estuary and saltmarsh – sometimes covered by sea water, sometimes by fresh water, and sometimes dry at low tide.*

THE MUDFLAT MILLIONS

The thick, dark, smelly mud that is uncovered at low tide around the estuary may not look very appetizing. Yet the few types of animals that are adapted to this strange and changing world have plenty of room and multiply in their millions.

The **ragworm** looks shaggy because of the bristles found along its sides. It is a wanderer, but sometimes makes a temporary burrow where it hides at low tide. As the water comes in, the worm emerges to hunt tiny animals such as shellfish and worms.

The **fiddler crab** from America lives in a burrow. When the sea retreats, the crab comes out to feed on tiny animals scooped from the mud. The male waves his huge claw to attract females and to defend his patch against other males.

The **mangrove tree** is at home on mudflats across the tropics. It can withstand salt water (at high tide) and fresh water (when it rains). At low tide, its roots 'breathe' air since they stick out of the airless mud like little sticks.

The **mudskipper** from Africa and Asia does not swim away with the retreating tide. This unusual fish can breathe in air, and also hold water in its gill chambers. It 'skips' across the mud on its front fins and retreats into a burrow for safety.

Who makes the marks?

Creatures like those in the picture on the left, and also estuary shellfish such as **cockles** and **clams**, make a good meal for wading birds. As they feed, the birds' bills leave marks in the mud. **Can you match these marks to their markers, and guess how the bird moves as it feeds?**

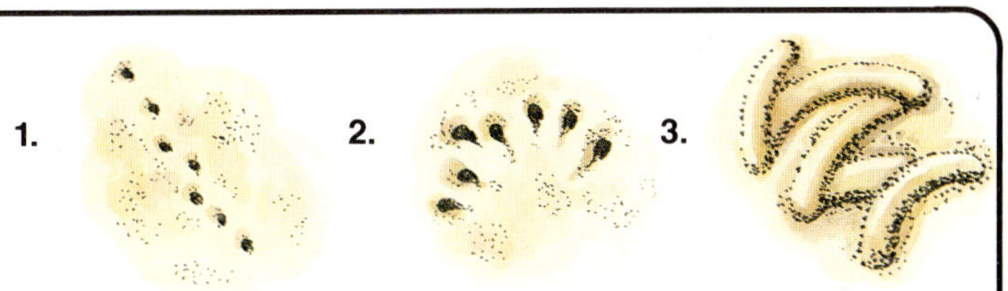

Sheldrake Broad, heavy bill for catching small, mud-dwelling creatures near the surface.

Sandpiper This small wader has a thin bill and jabs for little worms, snails and other titbits.

Curlew A large wader with a long, strong bill for probing deep down for crabs, worms, snails and other deeper-dwelling animals.

THERE AND BACK AGAIN

A few specialized animals are able to make the journey from fresh water to sea water – and even back again. The **Atlantic salmon's** eggs hatch in rivers far inland. After two or three years the young salmon swim to the sea. When they are adult and ready to breed, they swim back to the river in which they were spawned. This could mean a journey of around 1000 kilometres. This journey, which entails having to swim upstream against the flow of water, is an extraordinary feat.

ANSWERS

WHO MADE THE MARKS?

1. The **sandpiper** makes small holes in a line. It walks quickly along, its bill pecking continually into the mud like the needle of a sewing-machine.

2. The **curlew** stands in one place and makes medium-sized holes in an *arc* or part-circle.

3. The **sheldrake** makes these marks. It swings its broad bill from side to side, ploughing up food as it paddles about slowly.

When the tide comes in

The sea shows little of interest when looked at from above, except perhaps for a leaping fish or diving seabird. But along the sea's edge, the ups and downs of the tide reveal a glimpse of what goes on under the surface. Life on the shore itself is a peculiar and harsh one of constant change: underwater for half the time, and out of it for the other half.

TIDE OUT

A sandy beach at low tide looks deserted. There are just a few marks in the sand, perhaps some small holes, or squiggly casts, or the ends of papery tubes. But don't be fooled. The Underwater Explorer must be patient, and watch and wait.

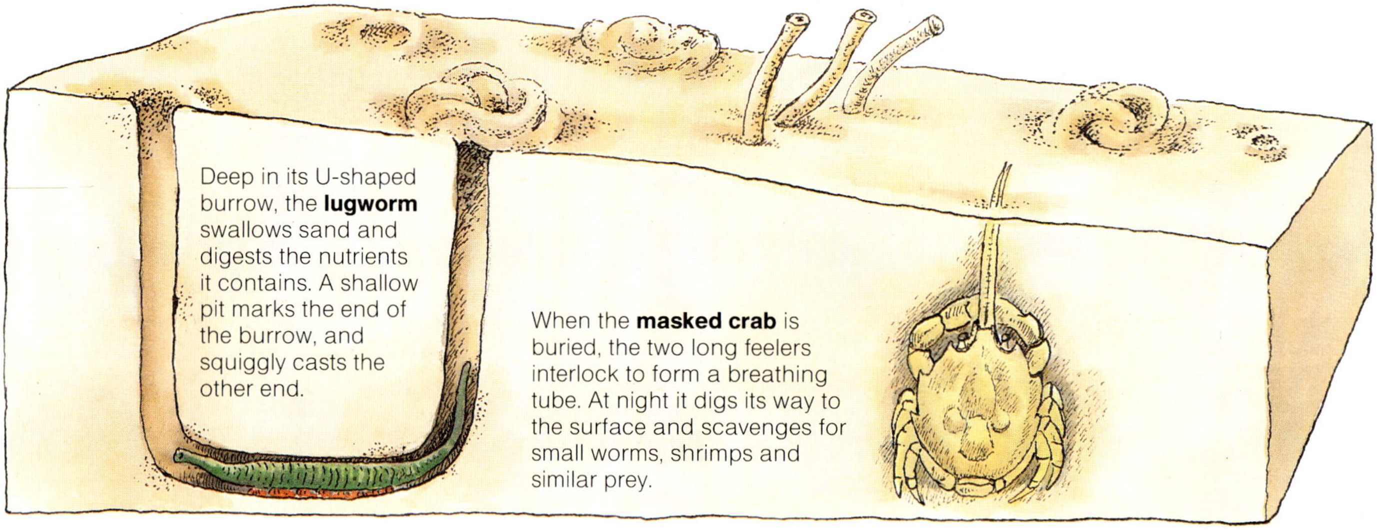

Deep in its U-shaped burrow, the **lugworm** swallows sand and digests the nutrients it contains. A shallow pit marks the end of the burrow, and squiggly casts the other end.

When the **masked crab** is buried, the two long feelers interlock to form a breathing tube. At night it digs its way to the surface and scavenges for small worms, shrimps and similar prey.

TIDE IN

As the sea returns, the submerged beach comes alive. Creatures emerge from holes, or extend their tentacles into the water, or open their shells to suck and sieve. Then, once again, the tide ebbs away, and they hide beneath the sand again.

The **cockle** opens the two parts of its shell and sticks out two frilly tubes called *siphons*. These are used to filter tiny pieces of food from the water.

The **peacock worm** lives in a tube of sand grains cemented together. It extends feathery tentacles that catch tiny bits of food floating past.

The **shrimp** 'tiptoes' over the sand at night, picking up small creatures in its spine-ended claws.

Make your own rockpool food web

Can you make these seaside rockpool animals into a 'food web' chart that shows who eats what? Trace each animal onto thick paper or poster board, colour it and cut it out. Arrange the cut-outs loosely in groups on a sheet of poster board: plants at the bottom, herbivores in the middle, carnivores on top, and scavengers to one side. Then move them around depending on what they eat, to make a food web. Stick them down and draw in arrows from food to feeder. **Which animal is top of the rockpool, the 'top carnivore'?** (Turn to page 36 to see if you've arrived at the right answer.)

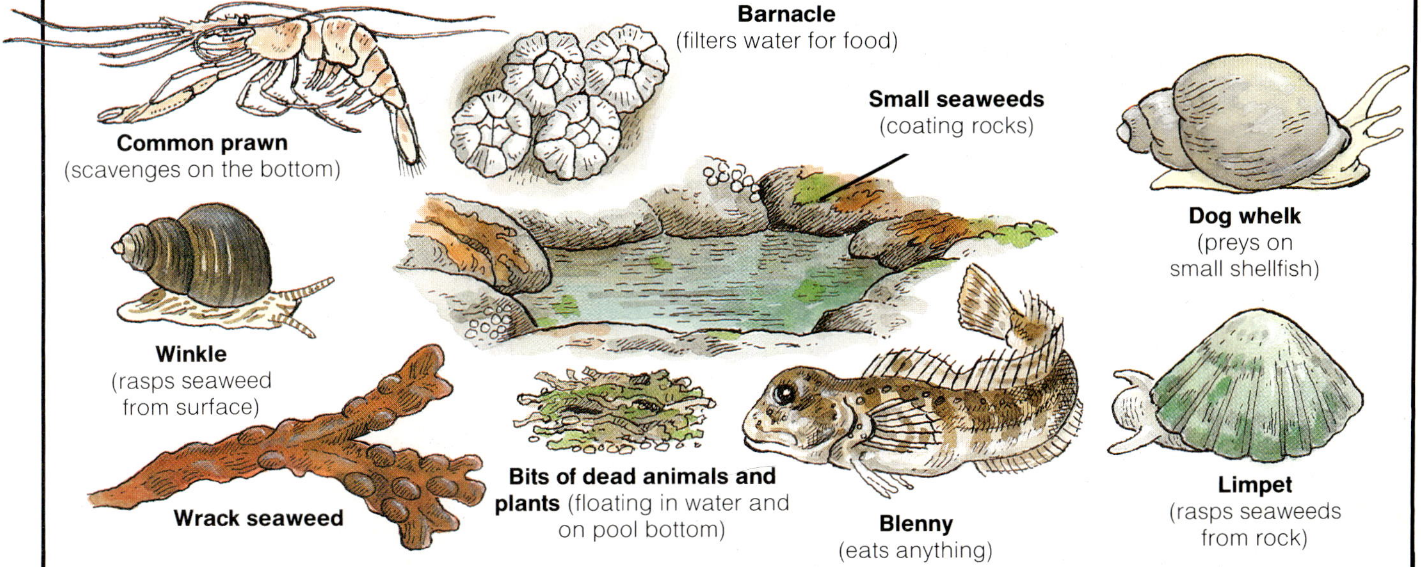

Whose babies?

Large animals like humans tend to notice other animals on the same scale – that is, other big animals. If you were only a few inches long, and floating in the sea, the world would look very different! Here are some of the tiny and strange creatures that might swim past you. They are the larval (young) forms of familiar seaside animals. **Can you guess which baby grows into which adult?**

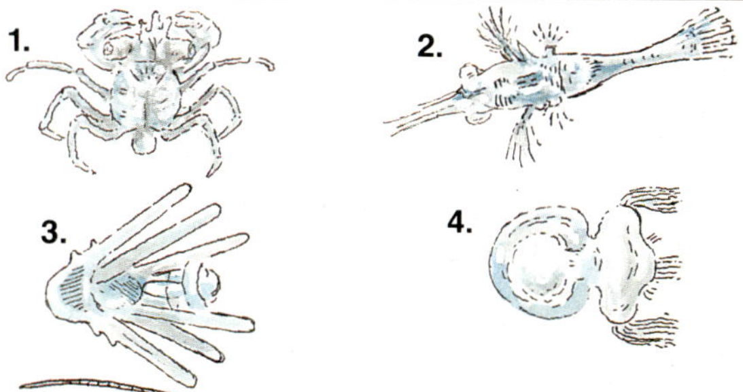

ANSWERS

WHOSE BABIES?

Baby 1 will grow into a **shore crab**. It already has the crab's two pincers and eight legs and the 'tail' will fold under the body.

Baby 2 will grow into a **prawn**. It has the prawn body shape and a long tail with 'fans' at the end.

Baby 3 will grow into a **sea urchin**. It is the only 'star-shaped' larva – the arms widen and fold over to make the urchin's ball-shaped body.

Baby 4 will grow into a **limpet**. The only baby with no legs at all, it has not yet developed its broad 'foot' and conical shell.

Coral community

The coral reef is the richest underwater habitat. Its tropical waters are warm and shallow, allowing plenty of sunlight for plant growth and ideal conditions for animal life. Like a tropical rainforest found on land, the reef teems with plants and creatures of all sizes. The fish that live here are dazzling in the brilliance and variety of their colours.

ANSWERS

WHO COUNTS AMONG THE CORAL?

1. is the brown **seahorse**. It can curl its tail around coral or plant stems, and swims by waving the dorsal fin on its back and its two *pectoral* (side) fins.

2. is a **blue-ringed octopus**. It is only 20 cm across, but its poisonous bite can kill a human.

3. is a **giant clam**, a huge relative of the cockle. Its fleshy 'lips' of vivid green, blue, red or purple are coloured by millions of microscopic algae living in the clam's tissues.

4. is a **sea anemone**. Although it looks like a grey and white flower, it's an animal related to corals and jellyfish. Its tentacles sting prey and pass it to the 'stomach' in its stalk.

5. is the orange **clownfish**. It lives among the anemone's tentacles without being stung, possibly because of a special mucus coating on its body. The fish benefits from its safe retreat and the anemone benefits from food dropped by the fish.

6. is the dark brown **stonefish**. If attacked, the fish can raise its spines and inject a strong venom into its attacker.

THE REEF-BUILDERS

Corals are tiny animals resembling miniature **sea anemones**. They live in groups and wave their tentacles in the water to catch microscopic floating food. The coral animals (called **polyps**) build stony, cup-shaped skeletons around their soft bodies for support and protection. When they die, more corals build new stony skeletons on top of the old ones. In this way, over hundreds of years, millions of skeletons pile on top of each other to form large rocks. This is the foundation of the coral reef.

Corals feed mainly at night. During the day they withdraw deep into their cups, showing only their faceless, stony skeletons. At night, they push their tentacles out to feed. In torchlight, the reef's surface shimmers in fantastic colours of red, blue, green and gold. Strangely, it is in the dark that the corals' colours are brightest.

My partner and I

On these two pages, there are two examples of living partnerships. In both of these examples the partners benefit in some way from the relationship. Biologists call this *symbiosis*. **Can you spot them?** (Turn to page 37 to see if you have the right answer.)

Who counts among the coral?

Different types of corals grow in fantastic shapes with lumps, branches, crevices and holes. These stony structures make excellent hiding places for all manner of reef creatures. **Can you spot six animals in this reef scene?** Not all are hiding – but they may not look like typical animals! Here are some clues-by-numbers:

1. is a fish with three fins and a curly tail

2. has eight arms and a deadly bite

3. has a two-part shell as big as a suitcase

4. has more than 100 stinging tentacles

5. hides in **4.** but doesn't get stung

6. has 13 poisonous spines – and looks like a stone

Life on the ocean wave

*Two-thirds of the Earth is covered by salt water. So a life on the ocean wave certainly means plenty of space. The surface layers of the seas are swarming with billions of tiny floating plants and creatures called **plankton**. The plant-plankton, or **phytoplankton**, need to capture the Sun's light energy in order to grow. So they can only exist in the top 90 metres of the sea near the surface. These plants are so numerous that they form nine-tenths of the plant life found in the sea – plants that sea animals rely on for food.*

BY-THE-WIND-SAILOR

This is not a true, single-animal jellyfish but a colony of several polyp animals living together. Some members of the colony make a gas that fills the 'float'. Others form the 'sail'. Those around the edge have stinging cells to catch small shrimps and other animals. Other polyps under the float digest the food and pass the nutrients to the rest of the colony.

GLAUCUS SEA SLUG

A not-too-distant relative of the slug that is found on land, this animal has pockets of gas in its digestive cavities and feathery 'feet'. It lives upside down at the surface of the water, feeding on jellyfish and similar prey.

BUBBLE-RAFT SEA SNAIL

Sometimes called the **violet** or **purple sea snail**, it makes air bubbles covered with *mucus*. The mucus hardens to form a rigid, raft-like float. The sea snail hangs upside down from this float and feeds on other floating creatures. It is especially fond of **By-the-wind-sailor jellyfish**.

Which one is different?

On these two pages are some creatures that live near the surface of the ocean. They all live underwater, but one of them cannot stay submerged forever. **Can you guess which one?** (There is a clue elsewhere on this page.)

REFRESHING SEA AIR

Phytoplankton absorb sunlight, carbon dioxide and minerals to make the nutrients on which they live. This process is called *photosynthesis*. One of the by-products of this process is oxygen, which all living things need in order to survive. Aquatic animals take oxygen from the water. At the same time a certain amount is given off for air-breathers, from ants to snakes, humans and whales.

ANSWERS

WHICH ONE IS DIFFERENT?

The **sea snail**, **sea slug**, **sunfish** and **jellyfish** are all truly underwater animals. The **sea snake** differs in one respect. Like other snakes, it breathes the oxygen in air, not the oxygen dissolved in water. So it must return to the surface to take a breath every now and then.

1. Glaucus sea slug
2. By-the-wind-sailor
3. Sea snail
4. Yellow-bellied sea snake
5. Sunfish

YELLOW-BELLIED SEA SNAKE

This snake is closely related to the cobras which live on land. It feeds, rests and breeds in the sea. It is about 71 cm long and swims by wriggling its body and waving its flattened, paddle-like tail. It has a poisonous bite and feeds on eels and small fish. Giant 'rafts' of sea snakes have been seen, many kilometres long, making this species probably the most numerous reptile on Earth.

SURFACE SUNBATHER!

One of the biggest surface-dwelling fish is the ocean **sunfish**. It may grow up to 4 metres long and weigh as much as 500 kg – that's heavier than six adult humans. It swims near the surface and sometimes lies on its side as though sunbathing. Whether its name comes from its round-bodied resemblance to a sun, or its sunbathing habit, is not clear.

Midwater world

*The middle zone of the ocean reaches from near the surface to several hundred metres down. It is here that the world's biggest fish live. The **basking shark** and **whale shark** cruise slowly along, their cavernous mouths open to filter plankton from the water. Besides these monsters, hundreds of other fish species make their home in the middle sea, as well as shrimps, squids and the great whales.*

HUNTERS OF THE MIDDLE SEA

Here are some of the fearsome predators of the middle sea. Each one comes from a different main animal group. One is a *mollusc* (a relative of octopuses and snails), one is a fish and one is a mammal. **Can you identify each one?**

The **sperm whale** is an 18-metre, 45-tonne monster with rows of sharp teeth for seizing squids, octopuses and fish. It must come to the surface to breathe, but it can then stay underwater for 90 minutes and dive down 3 kilometres.

The **great white shark** is the legendary 'man eater' (although it has attacked women as well!). At 6 metres long and 3 tonnes in weight, it is the biggest predatory fish.

The **giant squid** is the biggest of all *invertebrate* animals (those without backbones). It dwells in deeper waters and has a body more than 2 metres long, with arms 15 metres in length that seize victims such as fish.

ANSWERS

HUNTERS OF THE MIDDLE SEA
The **sperm whale** breathes air, so it is not a fish, but a mammal. The **giant squid** has 'arms' like an octopus, so it is a mollusc. The **great white shark** is, of course, a fish. However, sharks differ from other fish in that their skeletons are made of *cartilage* or gristle, not bone.

COLOURED FOR CAMOUFLAGE
The **plaice** is well camouflaged for its way of life. Lying on the ocean floor, its upper surface merges with the gravel, rocks and mud and become almost invisible. The underparts are white because they are usually never seen, being flat against the sea-bed. The fish does not use up valuable nutrients which would be needed to change the underside from its normal whitish flesh colour.

Record-breaker

The **blue whale** is the most massive animal ever to have lived on Earth. The biggest grow to nearly 30 metres long and weigh almost 200 tonnes. Such a huge body is possible only with the support and buoyancy of water. This great mammal feeds on shrimp-like creatures called **krill**. The whale sieves the krill from the water using the rows of baleen plates along each side of its mouth.

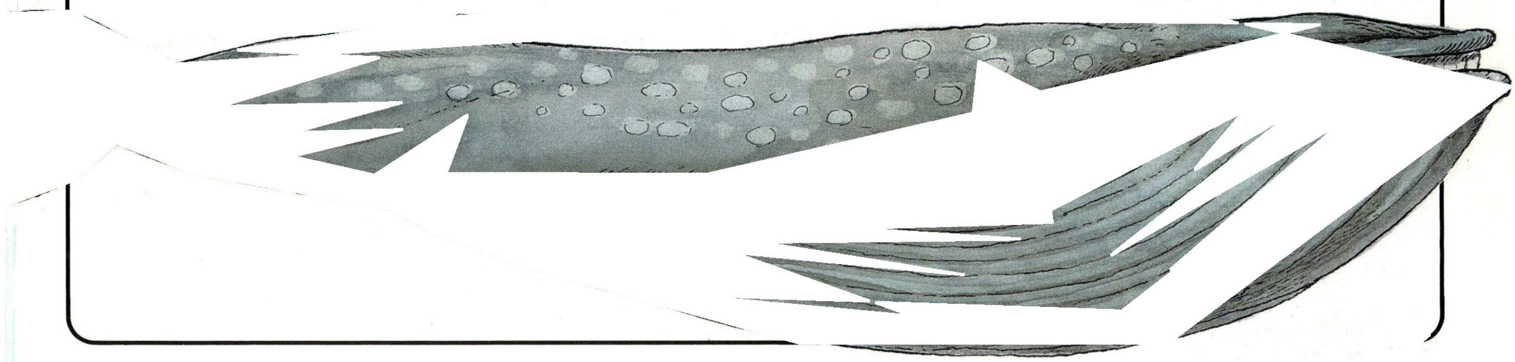

Coloured for camouflage

Many fish that swim in open, well-lit water, like the **sea bass**, have silvery underparts but a back that is grey, blue, or green. This form of colouration is called *countershading*, since it helps to counter (oppose) the usual effect of light from above casting shadows on an animal's underside. In this way the fish is *camouflaged* and cannot be easily seen by predators.

But what about the plaice, a type of flatfish? Why is it dark and speckly on its upper surface, yet white underneath?

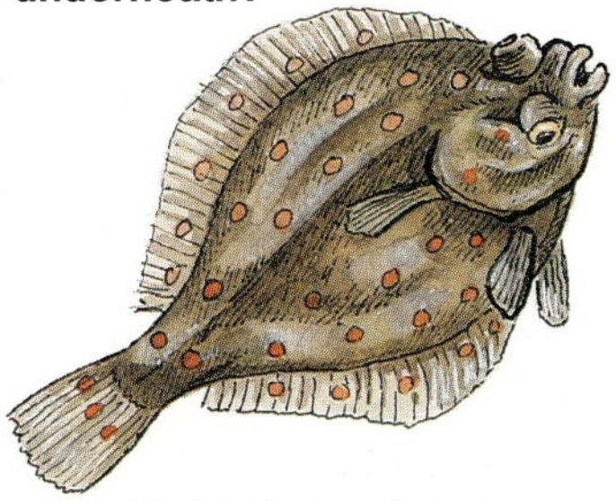

Plaice from above

Plaice from below

1. Without countershading
Seen from the side, light from above normally makes an animal's upper surface light and its underside dark.

2. With countershading
Light from above makes the dark back lighter, while the light belly becomes darker – and so the usual shadow effect is eliminated.

3. Seen from below
Looking up, the water's surface appears shining and silvery, and so does the fish's underside.

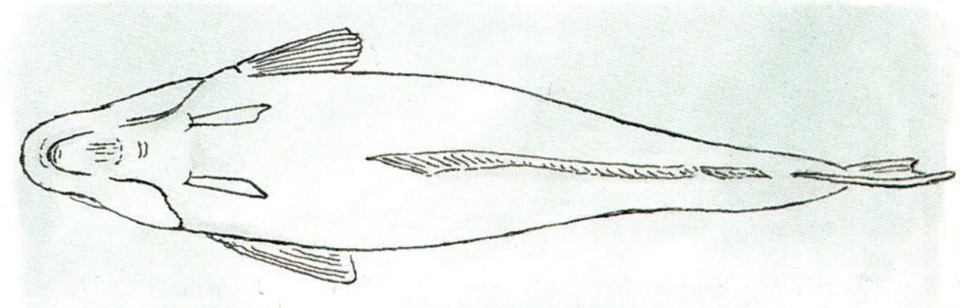

4. Seen from above
Looking down, the deeper water beneath appears dark (grey, blue, or green), and so does the fish's back.

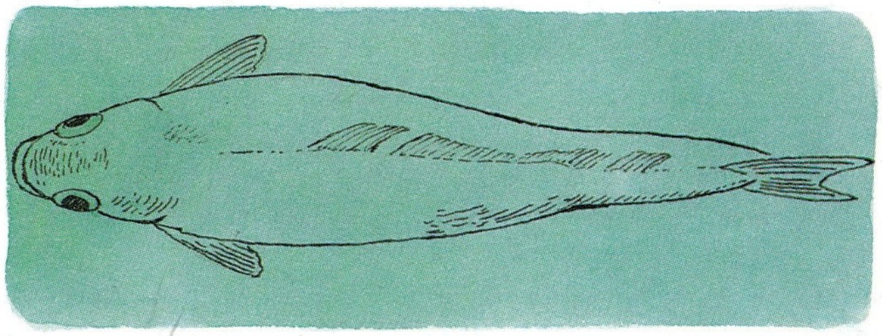

Life in deep water

It is difficult to grasp the immensity of the seas. In the centre of the Pacific Ocean water stretches for thousands of kilometres all around, and for thousands of metres above and below. In the blackness of its depths, there is not enough light for plants to grow. So animals must survive by eating the 'rain of remains' that floats down from above – or hunt each other. The temperature is about 3–5°C all year round, and hardly any currents disturb the stillness.

Lurer, gulper, or filterer?

These three strange creatures live in the depths of the oceans. Each one feeds in a different way, and each is similar to one of the animals featured on this page. **Can you figure out which is which?**

Sea lily Has feathery arms that wave in the water, and a stony 'stalk' that anchors it to the sea bed.

Lanternfish Has rows of 'lights' along its body that shine with a reddish glow.

Viper fish Long, thin fish with fangs like a snake. Comes near the surface at night and lives in the depths by day.

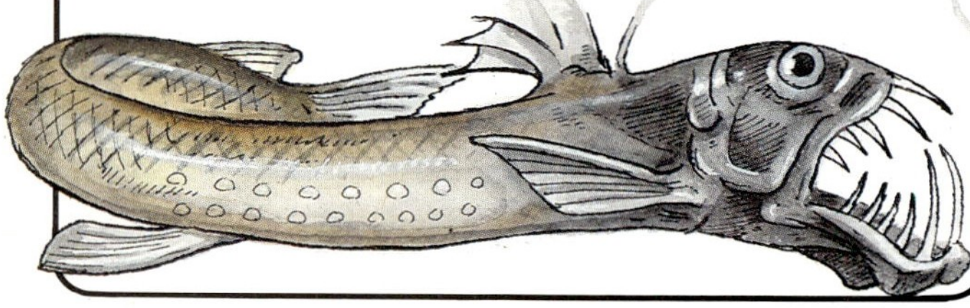

UNDERWATER VENTS

Scientists have always thought that all life on Earth is 'Sun-powered'. Plants capture the Sun's light energy and use it for growth; animals eat the plants and take in this energy; and so on, to form a food web (see page 23). But recently, scientists have discovered animals on the sea bed that get their

ANSWERS

LURER, GULPER, OR FILTERER?

The **sea lily** is a filter-feeder, like the **deep-sea cucumber**. It too is a relative of the starfish.

The **lanternfish** is a lurer, like the **anglerfish**. Rows of lights along its body are thought to attract smaller creatures, which it quickly swallows. The lights are also a signal to other lanternfish, when looking for a mate.

The **viper fish** is a gulper. Its mouth can open very wide and its sharp fangs make sure the victim does not escape.

The open sea at last! The bad chemicals and unnaturally warm water fade away. But the troubles are not over. High-pitched sound waves ping there way through the water and almost 'deafen' our traveller, who's made dizzy by their force.

Soon after, a swooshing sensation makes the underwater world tremble. A giant net sweeps past, crammed with distressed and dying fish. With a sprinting swim around the edge, our traveller manages to reach safety.

A great vibrating shape swirls past in the distance, its propellor turning ferociously. Then a shattering roar seems to split the sea apart. A dark shape heads up towards the surface, boiling the water around it, and disappears into the sky.

After months of swimming, our traveller arrives in the middle ocean. A dark cloud blots out the sunlight. Surface animals are in danger, coated with a thick, dark sticky substance that suffocates them. Will these perils never end?

ANSWERS

Our underwater traveller is the **salmon** (page 21).

Around the world, salmon have declined in numbers enormously. Looking at the perils we put in their way, it is not difficult to see why.

1. is a water-wheel and waterfall belonging to a watermill. Years ago it ground corn and wheat into flour, but today it's a tourist attraction.

2. is a hydro-electric dam, using the power of water to generate electricity. There is a small artificial stream called a 'salmon ladder' alongside the dam, but not all fish find it.

3. is a chemical factory pouring toxic (poisonous) wastes into the river. There are laws against such pollution.

4. is a power station built on the estuary. It takes in huge volumes of sea water to cool its generating equipment. The warmed water flows back into the sea as 'thermal pollution'.

5. is the sonar ('echo-sounder') of a trawler on the surface above. The sonar uses sound waves to locate large schools of fish (see page 33).

6. is the trawler's net, scooping up millions of sea inhabitants. Too much fishing has meant that many species of fish in our seas are now rare.

7. is a naval submarine on an underwater mission. It launches an underwater missile, which will rocket high into the air and eventually land thousands of kilometres away.

8. is an oil slick. It's not oil leaking from a tanker after an accident. It's from an oil tanker that has cleaned out its tanks and illegally released the oil into the sea.

Quiz time

There are many more things for you to discover in the mysterious underwater world of ponds, lakes, rivers and oceans. Here are a few more puzzles for you to solve. You can find out more from books, magazines and television – and by keeping your eyes open wherever you happen to be.

THE ROCKPOOL FOOD WEB

The rockpool food web of plants and animals from page 23 should look like this:

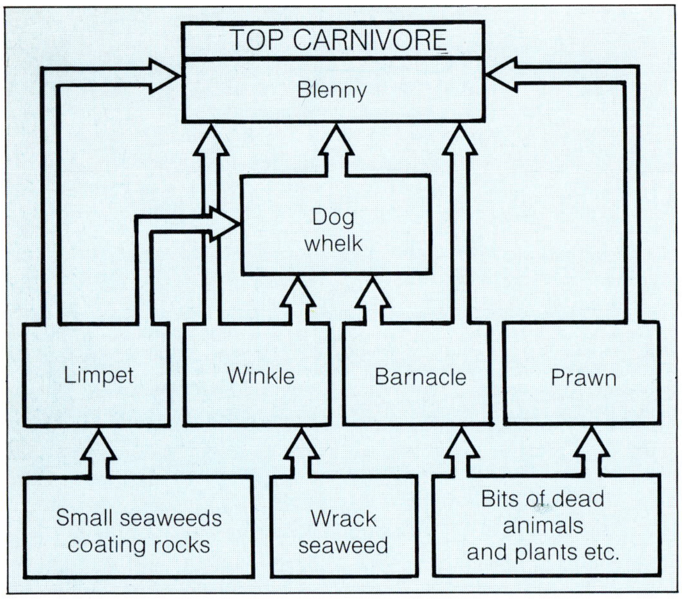

USEFUL PARTNERSHIP

The deep-sea giant clam has bacteria actually living in its flesh. The clam gives the bacteria a safe home, and feeds on some of the nutrients made by the bacteria. **Do you know what this type of relationship, which benefits both partners, is called?** (It is mentioned on another page in the book.)

Whose eggs ?

In spring, various animals come to the pond to breed. In the picture are three types of eggs. Each egg is like a spot in a small ball of jelly. But some are laid in large masses, some are laid singly, while some are in long thin strings. **Can you match the eggs to the amphibians that laid them?** Remember: you probably know about frog spawn, and **newts** lay small eggs!

SEA-WATER STRAINER

Herrings are sleek, silvery fish. They are about 40 cm long, and are so numerous that they are an important link in the food web of the oceans. Herrings 'strain' plankton from the water by means of comb-like inner edges on their gills, which work like sieves. In turn, they are eaten by larger fish such as **tuna**. We also join in the food web. About 3 million tonnes of these fish are caught each year in the Atlantic Ocean.

The same straining technique for food is used by another much bigger, sea creature mentioned elsewhere in the book. **Can you find out which one?**

THE NEED FOR WATER

People do not live underwater, but they need water. Look at a map, and try to figure out why towns and cities were built in the places they were. On this map of China, notice how all the big cities were built on or near . . . **what, and why?**

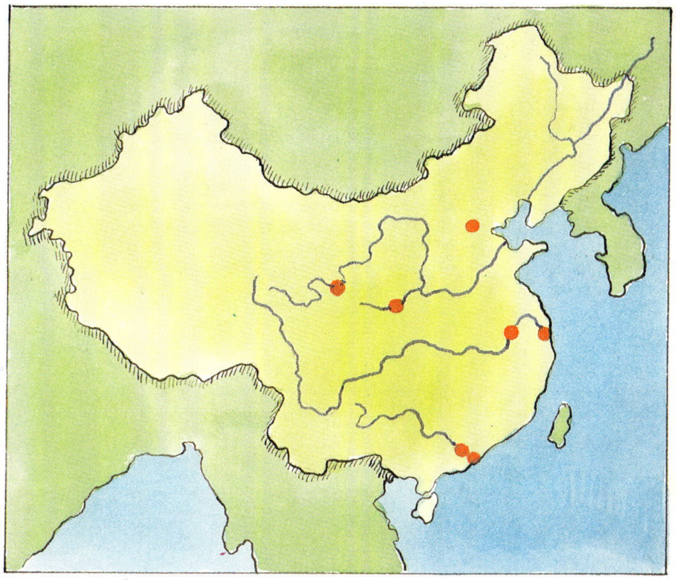

China's major cities are either on the coast or on large rivers (or both!) People need water for drinking, washing, cooking and transport. Today, wells can be drilled and cars, trains and planes carry people far inland. Can you find a modern city that is not near the sea or a large river? (Look at a map of Brazil, Brasilia, the capital, was only founded in 1960.)

ANSWERS

USEFUL PARTNERSHIP?
The type of relationship where the clam benefits the bacteria, and the bacteria help the clam, is called *symbiosis*. For other examples, including the giant clam of coral reefs, see pages 24–25.

MY PARTNER AND I
The giant clam has algae in its tissues which provide it with nutrients. In return, the algae have a safe place to live. This kind of relationship is called symbiosis. The clownfish and the anemone have a similar kind of relationship. The anemone provides the fish with protection, while the anemone feeds on particles of food dropped by the fish.

SEA-WATER STRAINER
The herring strains tiny plants and animals from the water – and so do the enormous whales. The herring's mouth is only about 5 cm long. The whale's is 6 metres long, and gulps many tonnes of water at a time. The water is sieved through the whale's 300 brush-like baleen plates.

WHOSE EGGS?
Many people are familiar with the great masses of spawn that appear in ponds each spring. These are the **frog's** eggs. Each female frog may lay over 2,000 eggs. The **toad** lays the 'necklace' of eggs, which might be 3 metres long and contain over 3,000 eggs. The **newt** lays each of her 200–300 eggs separately. She wraps it in the leaf of a water plant to hide and protect it.

INDEX